2007

MATT KENSETH

Marcus Figorito

PowerKiDS press™

New York

Published in 2007 by The Rosen Publishing Group, Inc.
29 East 21st Street, New York, NY 10010

Book Design: Michael J. Flynn

Photo Credits: Cover (Kenseth) © Jamie Squire/Getty Images; cover (background), pp. 5, 9 ©
Robert Laberge/Getty Images; p. 7 © Darrell Ingham/Getty Images; pp. 11, 19 © Jonathan Ferrey/
Getty Images; pp. 13, 17, 21 © Rusty Jarrett/Getty Images; p. 15 © Craig Jones/Getty Images.

Library of Congress Cataloging-in-Publication Data

Figorito, Marcus.
  Matt Kenseth / Marcus Figorito.
      p. cm. — (NASCAR champions)
  Includes bibliographical references and index.
  ISBN-13: 978-1-4042-3458-6
  ISBN-10: 1-4042-3458-6 (lib. bdg. : alk. paper)
 1. Kenseth, Matt—Juvenile literature. 2. Automobile racing drivers—United States—Biography—
Juvenile literature. I. Title. II. Series.
  GV1032.K455F54 2007
  796.72092—dc22
  (B)
                                    2006014606

Manufactured in the United States of America

Contents

Matt Kenseth is a race car driver. He races stock cars.

5

Matt used to fix his dad's stock car. His dad gave him the car when Matt turned 16.

7

Matt won the third race he entered. He was only 16 years old!

8

9

Matt started driving full-time in NASCAR's top series in 2000. He was the NASCAR Rookie of the Year that year.

10

Matt won a NASCAR championship in 2003.

2003
NASCAR WINSTON CUP CHA...
MATT KENSETH

13

Matt drove in five all-star races in 2004. This means he was one of the best NASCAR drivers.

15

Matt won three of the all-star races. He won a lot of money!

17

Matt raced in more all-star races in 2005 and 2006.

18

19

Matt is still one of the best drivers in NASCAR. He has many fans.

Glossary

all-star (ALL–STAHR) One of the best at a sport or activity.

championship (CHAM-pea-uhn-ship) A contest held to see who is the best in a sport.

rookie (RU-kee) Someone who is in their first year in a sport.

series (SEER-ees) A number of things or events of the same kind that happen one after another.

stock car (STAHK KAHR) A race car that looks like the cars people drive on the road.

22

Books and Web Sites

Books

Buckley, James. *NASCAR.* New York: DK Children, 2005.

Buckley, James. *Speedway Superstars.* Pleasantville, NY: Reader's Digest, 2004.

Web Sites

Due to the changing nature of Internet links, PowerKids Press has developed an online list of Web sites related to the subject of this book. This site is updated regularly. Please use this link to access the list:
http://www.powerkidslinks.com/NASCAR/kenseth/

23

Index